© 2007 Kyle Cassidy

Published by

krause publications
An Imprint of F+W Publications

700 East State Street • Iola, WI 54990-0001
715-445-2214 • 888-457-2873
www.krausebooks.com

Our toll-free number to place an order or obtain
a free catalog is (800) 258-0929.

Colophon

The body font is Centaur, designed over a period of four years and finished in 1915 by Bruce Rogers,
one of the greatest American type designers. It is considered one of his masterpieces. The Monotype
foundry issued the font in 1929. It is based on a font designed in by Nicholas Jensenit in 1470.

The headline fonts are Engravers Gothic and Franklin Gothic Book. Engravers Gothic is a beautiful
but simple font designed by Olga Chaeva for ParaType in 1999. Franklin Gothic Book is a geometric
sans serif designed by Sol Hess between 1936 and 1947 and issued by Monotype.

Library of Congress Catalog Number:
2007923000

ISBN: 978-0-89689-543-0

Designed by Kyle Cassidy & Thomas Nelsen

Edited by Paul Kennedy

Printed in China

ACROSS AMERICA

Have nothing in your houses that you do not know to be useful or believe to be beautiful.

William Morris (1834–1896)
Hopes and Fears for Art (1882)

Travel is fatal to prejudice, bigotry and narrow-mindedness, and many of our people need it sorely on these accounts.
Broad, wholesome, charitable views of men and things can not be acquired by vegetating in one little corner of the earth all one's lifetime.

Mark Twain (1835-1910)
The Innocents Abroad (1869)

You can drive for a day and a half across West Texas and not see anything you didn't see the mile before: creosote, scrub brush, mesquite, the occasional shin-dagger agave. The wheels spin under your car, the speedometer hovers over numbers never seen by drivers in the Eastern states and still, the horizon seems no closer.

To say I was unprepared for West Texas is being generous. Standing on the asphalt in the middle of the road I can see for miles — the road is like a line drawn on the wide, blank landscape with a giant pencil, as straight and unending as Euclidian geometry. I'm at least a day behind schedule and there's no escape from the sun which at the moment is baking my brain like a pie. My lips have split open from

dehydration despite the fact that I've been drinking water as fast as I thought humanly possible. But, watching the heat rise off the silent highway, I realize this is about as good as life can get.

And as bad as it was, it wasn't the worst weather I'd ever experienced.

I'd been to Jacksonville Florida one July about fifteen years before, visiting friends. It was the most inhospitable place I could possibly imagine. People would sit forlornly inside their houses and draw straws to see who had the unenviable task of rushing out to the driveway to start the car, turn on the air conditioner and race back to the house where everyone else would splash them with water and ice as they collapsed through the door. It was exactly as I imagined life on the surface of the sun would be, if the surface of the sun had 97% humidity all the time. The difference between Florida and West Texas though is that in West Texas you might be 300 miles from the nearest air conditioner.

In the summer of 2006 I loaded myself, two cameras, four lenses, and a suitcase full of clothes into my assistant Phil Forrest's 1992 Jeep Cherokee with no air conditioning and we started off across the desert to photograph gun owners in their homes. By this point I'd already found a publisher and there was word-of-mouth buzz about the book making it relatively easy for me to find people in every town we stopped in. Despite the fact that I was, for the most part, just starting out, all this conspired to give me the sensation that I was well on my way.

JUST WHAT IS IT WITH AMERICANS AND GUNS?

At a dinner party two years earlier I found myself sitting next to a former presidential campaign staffer. Conversation fell to the election and he mentioned that part of his job had been to help wrangle the "gun vote" — which I found fascinating. I'd never really thought about the "gun vote" much less how it would be wrangled. And indeed, this was a murky area, even for professionals. Nobody was exactly sure how big the "gun vote" was; all anybody could do was guess. The National Rifle Association (NRA), the country's largest pro-gun lobbying group, quotes the Bureau of Alcohol, Tobacco, Firearms and Explosives (BATFE) estimate that in 1999 there were about 215 million guns in America and at least one gun in about half of the households in the country. The Brady Campaign (the nation's leading anti-gun coalition) estimates there are 192 million guns in America, owned by 39% of the population.

Whether it's 39% or 50% of Americans, it's still an awful lot of people. I started wondering just who they were, what they looked like, and how they lived. And there, somewhere between the main course and desert, was the genesis of this project.

When I first started, I was photographing people in my studio with very careful attention to lighting and detail. After a few months of intermittent work, I had a series of really nicely lit shots that all looked the same and, ultimately, left us none the wiser about why so many people had so many guns. I knew I was no closer to my goal and that if I really wanted anything substantial I'd have to start over.

Few things tell our stories as quickly and succinctly as our homes — our living spaces, our books, our movies, our pets, and our teapot collections. The things that we surround ourselves with and the way we place them are reflections of our inner selves and a window into our truth. It dawned on me that what I really needed was to photograph people in their homes.

I love being inside people's houses. I love seeing what they have on their shelves, the photos on the mantle, whether they have trash on the floor or unopened bars of soap in the bathroom, and I like meeting people. In a lot of ways, I really think this was the perfect project. Each subject was unique, each was its own particular challenges of lighting and composition, I was on the road, meeting a lot of really interesting people whom I might never have crossed paths with otherwise, apart from the weather, everything was good.

I made two decisions early on: First I would photograph anyone who was willing, owned a gun, and whom I could physically get to: I didn't want the temptation of starting to cherry pick people for their opinions or because they had some huge gun collection. Secondly, I decided I wouldn't treat these subjects any differently than I would if I were photographing portraits of lottery winners — I didn't want to rely on the crutch of controversy to prop my images up. I wanted a good portrait first.

I always thought that you couldn't "discover" a place if there were people already living there when you arrived. But later I realized that travel isn't always about the place, that the discovery is about you. Christopher Columbus might not have discovered America, but he learned an awful lot about Christopher Columbus 29 days out of sight of land.

The great American story has always been about travel and exploration. When Horace Greeley advised "Go West, young man," he was pointing to millions of square miles of opportunity and places that very few, if any, people had set foot. The American story was always about moving, going, finding — dispersing from high densities to low ones.

This place, all of it, was originally Someplace Else and nearly all the people here now are from Someplace Else. At most we have a 500 year history. Which is nothing. There are cakes in Italy older than that. When the Pilgrims landed at Plymouth Rock the Parthenon had been standing for a 1,000 years, the Pyramids 3,000 more. The world laughs at 500 years. So what makes this place any different?

"It took Moses 40 years to cross the Sinai," my college roommate once remarked, "I did it in two hours." He paused, and then added, almost incidentally, looking around the room, "but I was on a bus." This comment rang true while I looked at maps of America. I'd crossed it dozens of times, from end to end, but always at 30,000 feet. I'd seen the Grand Canyon all at once, and 300 miles of the Ohio River the same way. But I hadn't sat at a bus stop in Woonsocket, Rhode Island, or done my laundry in Monkey's Eyebrow, Tennessee. So what did I know about America?

When it was all behind me, I'd traveled 15,000 miles over two years asking people one question: *"Why do you own a gun?"*

In this text, people and animals are listed from left to right. All guns are identified as completely as possible.

— *Kyle Cassidy*
Philadelphia,
January 1, 2007

Why do you own a gun?

CICILY AND ROB WITH KOOKIE
WISCONSIN

.22 Savage, .22 Remington, Eastern Arms 20 ga., Remington 12 ga, Mossberg 12 ga, Savage 270, Winchester 12 ga, HK USP H5, Ruger Single 6 (.22)

Cicily: I grew up in a gun environment, but the only people who had guns were gang members. I thought guns were bad things and only bad people had them. I had no exposure to any positive gun experiences so I didn't know there were normal people who had guns. Matt took me shooting and I had so much fun. I was really impressed by how responsible everybody was. I felt like I was part of something very serious, fun, but everyone took it so seriously and so responsibly that I felt very safe. Now I want to go small game hunting because I love to cook. I want to learn how to cook pheasant and rabbit. I want to learn how to butcher — I want to do it all. All the stuff that all these old Wisconsin women seem to have been born knowing.

Rob: I went through hunter safety when I was younger. The only time we ever saw guns was during hunting season. Then during college, there was a place where you could rent guns and go target shooting. My friends and I started target shooting and it really went from there. Now it's just become a really enjoyable pastime. Anybody who likes darts or pool or especially golf, anything like that would also enjoy target shooting.

Aaron with Callie
Kentucky

91/30 Mosin Nagant, Yugo SKS, Remington 870

It originally started out as hunting, that became target shooting, and in the Marine Corps I got into distance shooting. The Mosen Nagant's my distance shooter; the SKS is my fun shooter; and the Remington 870 is my do-all. I have a turkey barrel. I have short barrel I use for home defense and skeet shooting. It works well for both. Everything has a purpose.

AARON AND BRITTNY
PENNSYLVANIA

Keltec Sub 2000, Glock 34, Glock 19, and Ruger Mark II

Aaron: My parents taught me to shoot, growing up in Utah. I got a gun here because we live in kind of a rough neighborhood and I take the subway home from work. I figured that since the bad guys had guns, I should have one, too.

Brittny: After practicing together and getting better, target shooting turned into a fun hobby that we could share.

VALERI AND ANDREW WITH ROMI
PENNSYLVANIA

CZ 40, BT99 Trap

Andrew: I started shooting trap when I was 15. I've just kept up with it.

ASHLEY
GEORGIA

Springfield 1911 .45

There are few things that beat a good day at the gun range, but the biggest reason I own firearms is because it's my right as a citizen of the United States of America and I refuse to take my rights for granted. Anyone that reads any history at all knows how dangerous that can be.

BILL AND CHRISTY WITH DAISY
WISCONSIN

Marlin 1895 MR - .450 Marlin, Ruger Vaquero - .44-40 cal

Bill: To preserve American heritage for future generations. By exercising the Second Amendment, you are guaranteeing future generations the right to self-preservation and guarding against government tyranny. The rights we lose as Americans are those we carelessly give away. If we give away the right to own firearms, the rest of the Bill of Rights won't be far behind. As far as I'm concerned, the Second Amendment should have been the first.

AUSTEN WITH CHARLOTTE
WISCONSIN

Winchester Model 88, .308

My dad had guns and hunted. My grandpa had some, and when he passed away I got a couple of his. I haven't gone hunting yet and I haven't decided if I will or not. Right now I'm happy with just target practice.

BARBARA AND RYAN WITH MAUSER AND STAR
PENNSYLVANIA

Ruger 10/22 Stainless, Keltek P32, Browning A-Bolt 270

Barbara: I own a handgun for self-defense. I own a rifle for target shooting. I have both because I live in the best country in the world and have the right as an American citizen. When we were first married, I was a bit hesitant to have a gun in the house because I wasn't used to it. Then I went to the range with Ryan several times and I realized how responsible he was with firearms. And as I became familiar with guns, I changed my mind.

Ryan: My father served in the second World War and taught me at a young age that freedom often comes with a high price. I own a gun because it's my God-given right as a citizen of the greatest country ever, the United States of America. God bless America!

AVERY
OREGON

Sig 226, Taurus .357, Mossberg 500, AK-47

It started out as a childhood fascination and kind of went from there. I started out collecting photographs and making drawings of guns — it's just ones of those things; from fascination to ownership. There are a lot of people who assume that because you own guns you're more of a violent person — I don't believe that.

Barbara with Samson and Delilah
Pennsylvania

Ruger Mark I

My dad took me target shooting when I was a kid, but I was so small all I got to do was pull the rifle trigger. As an adult I really enjoy target shooting and am attracted to the energy and feeling of self-empowerment.

JENNIFER, CHRIS AND DANIEL
WASHINGTON

AR-15, Remington 870, M1A, Colt MK IV

Jennifer: I'd say for home security. Keeps us safe, or makes us feel safe as long as we are responsible with it. Especially with our 2-year old son, to keep the guns safe. Then everybody is happier and protected.

Chris: One of the primary reasons I own a gun is because, thanks to our founding fathers and the writing of the Constitution and the Bill of Rights, it is our God-given right under the Second Amendment. My family has owned guns ever since I can track back through probably about ten generations, so I guess it's kind of a family tradition and the fact it's our right.

Bennett with Opus
Massachusetts

17th Century Horse Pistols

As a kid I earned my NRA Sharpshooter badge, owned several air rifles, shot with a Remington .22 pump and collected antique firearms. As an adult I believe that in 21st century America we should outlaw handgun ownership, and strictly control long-gun ownership. I think owning a handgun for self-protection is specious reasoning. All you have to do is compare the number of documented cases there are each year of handguns actually providing protection, versus how many children and adults die each year in accidents and intentional shootings with legally owned handguns. I've kept my great grandfather's horse pistols. They make a nice lamp.

MATT AND CATIE WITH NILES
WISCONSIN

Ruger 10-22, Steyr M9, Beretta Neos .22, Mosin-Nagant M44

Matt: I didn't come from an anti-gun family, just a family that didn't have guns. I heard about some friends who were going shooting and thought I should give that a shot, literally. So I went down to a local range — then I bought my own gun. And another. And another. And another. I don't do anything aside from target shoot. It's a good time.

Catie: I like to go shooting. It's fun. I also feel a lot safer with a gun in the house. Matt went up north to a bachelor party once and took all the guns with him. I was sitting alone in the apartment, suddenly realizing how vulnerable I felt.

Bash with Cisco

Bushmaster Carbon AR-15

I just think it's a good thing to have.

B.A. WITH ANNIE
ARIZONA

Glock 17

I used to want to be a police officer. That's what sparked my interest in guns. I started shooting at shooting matches and I enjoyed that. I own a gun for protection and because I like to shoot. My parents — you wouldn't catch them owning guns. My mom, at first she wasn't too thrilled: *You can't bring your gun into my house* and that sort of thing. I have a concealed carry permit and she doesn't ask. Out of sight, out of mind.

Jerry and Colin
New Jersey

Browning Citori

Jerry: We are our own last line of defense. I haven't seen a compelling argument from the anti's as to why law abiding citizens shouldn't have guns. I think we all agree that criminals shouldn't have them; but what's the advantage of taking guns from good people?

Colin: My dad taught me to shoot when I was 5 or 6 and it's how we still spend time together. He's a terrible golfer, but he's a great shot. We've definitely bonded over the years shooting sporting clays. What's the alternative? You go over to visit, barbecue and watch TV?

CHRIS WITH LOIS
MISSOURI

Mossberg 500

I can't think of a good reason not to own a gun. My mother's English and would never have one in the house — maybe that's why I own a lot of guns. Either that or I'm just crazy. That could be it, too.

CHRIS AND CECILIA
PENNSYLVANIA

Ravin Arms .25 & Six Gun Tattoos

Chris: I don't promote the fact that I have a gun, but I grew up in Maine. I don't believe in hunting. I'll still eat the meat, but I don't want to kill anything.

Cecilia: I grew up in Rappahannock County — the land of very big trucks and very big guns. The gun trading post is right across the street from the church.

BILLY
MISSOURI

Amadro Rossi .45 Long Colt

I was in the Marines and then the Army. I like to sport shoot and competition shoot. I started actually collecting guns about two years ago.

PATRICK WITH KURO KUMA
PENNSYLVANIA

HK .40 cal, Sig Sauer .380

Protection. I work in the night club industry, and I'm a personal bodyguard. Guns are part of my profession.

Diego and Nakita with Fiona
Pennsylvania

CE TME, Marlin, Springfield XD - .45

Diego: If there ever comes a time when I have to defend my life, I wouldn't trust that to anybody else — no matter what oath they took or what contract they signed. I came to America from Brazil. The Second Amendment, I think, is one of the best things about this country.

Nakita: I grew up in Russia. My dad always had guns in his closet. I always knew where they were, how to use them, always ready in case of an emergency — if anything imposed my life or my relatives, I would be ready to use it.

Danielle with Zeke
Pennsylvania

Glock 26

My father was a Philadelphia police officer for over 30 years — 20 plus of those years were spent in the Homicide Division. I remember stepping over his gun every night on the stairs on my way to bed. You didn't mess with Daddy's gun — it wasn't a toy. Growing up the daughter of a cop you learn early on that the world can be a dangerous place and that you need to be able to protect yourself, should you have to.

Christina and Keary with Clio and Evey
New Mexico

Fedord M-14a, Imbel/Enfield L1A1, Imbel STG-58, Mossberg 500, Ishapore ZA1 Jungle Carbine, Arisaka Type 38, Enfield #1 Mk3, Enfield #4 Mk2, Mosin Nagant M91/30, Tula SKS, Romak AK-47, Glock 35, Glock 26, Webley MK4, Star Model BM, CZ 27

Christina: I've always been interested in guns, and shooting them and becoming proficient in it. I collect World War II guns.

Keary: Firearms are the last tangible pieces of military history for people to collect and enjoy. Other things such as uniforms and the soldiers themselves will be long gone — these guns will still be firing in 100 years.

BRANDON
OREGON

Makarov PA 63

Weapons are a matter of personal sovereignty and the Left needs to be armed too, just like the Right. Throughout the long history of imperialism in the world, if indigenous peoples were as equally armed during attempts at colonization then history would be completely different.

DAVID
PENNSYLVANIA

Mossberg M44 "Us Gov't" training rifle - .22, SVT-40 7.62x54mm, K-98 Mauser - 8mm, G-43 Walther - 8mm, M1 Carbine - .30 cal, Walther P-38 - 9mm, Kimber Eclipse - .45 cal, Ruger GP-100 - .357 magnum, H+K P2000 - .40 cal, AK-47 - 7.62 x 39mm, AK-74 - 5.45 x39mm, Bushmaster M4A3 - 5.56 x 45mm, Ruger M77/22 - .22 cal, Erma MP-40 - 9mm

My family has a rich heritage of gun ownership and military service. I grew up with guns in the house and having fun shooting with my father. I want to pass those skills on to my daughter so she will be able to defend herself from any threat.

As an Army officer I swore to protect this nation and its freedoms from all enemies, foreign and domestic. In my home, these are the tools that I would depend on to defend myself and my family. Gun ownership is a constitutional right and an inherent good for law-abiding citizens. I am proud that I fought in the war on terror to keep this right alive for centuries to come.

David and Tara with Raven
Pennsylvania

Glock 29 10mm and Savage 12 gauge pump

David: We are our first line of defense. In the extremely unlikely event that we are the victims of an attempted violent crime, we are both trained and ready to protect our family and property from harm. I can't suggest strongly enough that if you take on the responsibility of firearms ownership, you take appropriate classes in safe gun handling and armed self-defense. We belong to a wonderful indoor range and are constantly taking new people with us to give shooting a try in a safe, clean, and friendly environment. Every single person we take ends up having a really good time. We've changed quite a few peoples' negative views of firearms this way.

Tara: Originally, I was scared of guns and everything they represented. After meeting David and his family, I became educated about how they are made and what makes them work. Instead of being fearful, I decided to try shooting one myself, and now I am hooked. It's a plus that my closest friends enjoy shooting, too. It's a way we bond.

DAN
PENNSYLVANIA

Mossberg Model 88, Bushmaster AR-15, Rock Island Armory / Sendra M16, Remington 700 PSS, Springfield XD, FN Five-seveN, HK USP, Sig Sauer P226, Colt Commander 1911, and Glock 22

I consider the ownership of arms not only a right, but the duty of a free people to themselves and future generations.

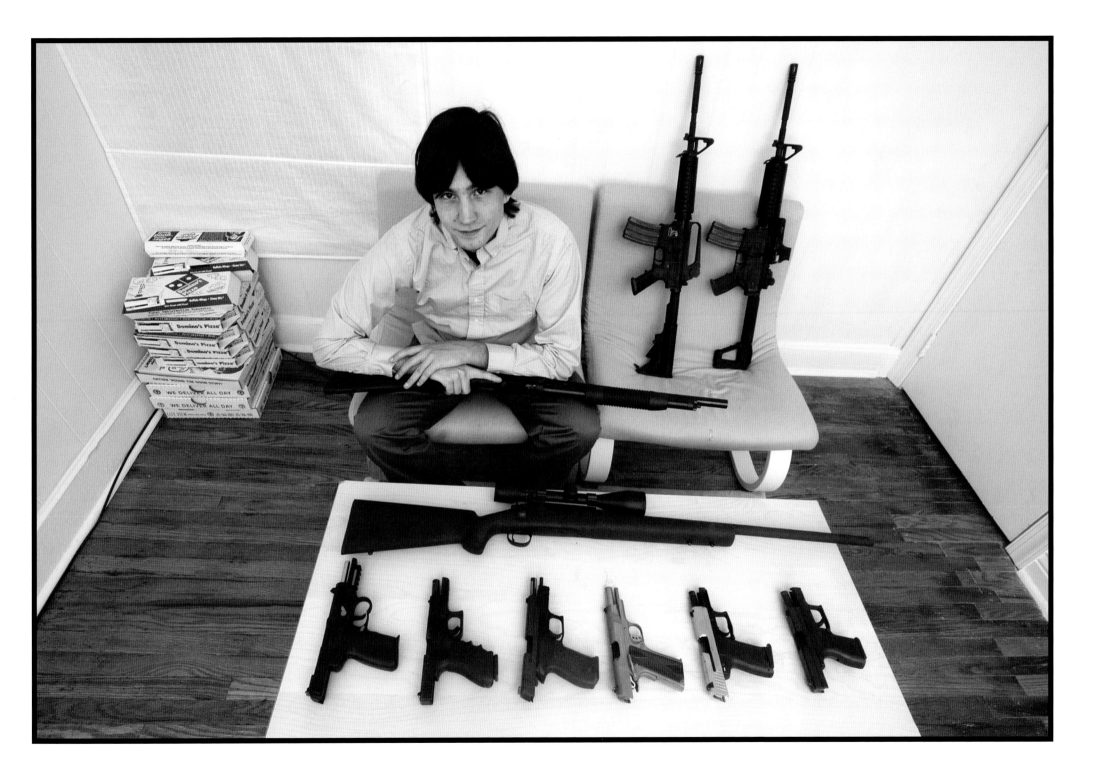

Uzi, Judi and Donno
Pennsylvania

Remington 870 Express HD, AK-47 SSR 85 C2

Donno: I own guns for the same reason I own fire extinguishers — while I certainly don't expect or hope for a worst case scenario, should one present itself, I'm prepared to take an active role in ensuring that my family survives. I grew up with guns in the house that were used regularly to put food on our table. I've known gun safety inside and out since I was a child. I'm confident my son will grow up with the same understanding and handle them with the same respect and care … whether he chooses to own guns or not.

Judi: I grew up in the South and I come from a family of hunters. One of my first memories is learning to shoot a gun in my backyard. When I moved to Philadelphia, I quickly realized that I wanted to buy a gun for home defense. The bottom line is if someone is threatening my child or me, I want to be able to protect us. My shotgun will take care of any intruder and I know how to use it.

CHRISTOPHER
OREGON

Glock 22

My father taught me to shoot and I grew up shooting.

DODD
KENTUCKY

AK-47, Mossberg 500

The shotgun is for home defense. I keep it under the bed. The idea, hopefully, is that I'll never have to fire it because just the sound of it racking in the dark will be enough to scare someone off. The AK was more of an impulse. I bought it at a gun show. I had a handgun too, but it was stolen out of my car. I did report that to the police.

EMERY AND PHIL WITH HUNTER
WISCONSIN

.30-06, .357, 44-mag, Desert Eagle, .44 mag, Benelli M1 Super 90 12 Gauge

Emery: I love to hunt.

Phil: I hunt and target shoot. Home protection is what I have my wife for.

HOWARD
PENNSYLVANIA

C. Sharps Arms Co. Model 1874 in .45-70

I love history and I love old mechanical devices — guns are both. I also enjoy target shooting.

DREW
MISSOURI

Sharps M-1874 45/70

I became a policeman because I grew up in a pretty bad area and I didn't like the policemen I saw. I thought that I could do better. Being in law enforcement, I've been able to buy guns from other policemen and I love the stories behind each one. Every gun I own has a lot of sentimental value for me.

AVERY, MILES, GREGG AND THERESA WITH GINNY
ARIZONA

Supressed Ruger 10-22's, M1 Garand, Two AR-15's–One Supressed

Gregg: The people who are anti-gun can name instance after instance, situation after situation, where a gun would do you no good — and I would agree with them. But if there's that hundred and first time, one time out of a 101 where having a gun would have meant saving your own child — you would sell your soul, or trade everything you have, to do that.

Theresa: Years ago I saw a burglar on television who said that his greatest fear was a homeowner with a gun and that if a homeowner even just pointed a gun at him, he'd surrender. And if he knew that a house had a gun in it, he wouldn't rob it. And, in fact, that's how he was caught — a woman pulled a gun on him while he was robbing her house. I wouldn't want to be in a situation where I needed a gun to protect my family and didn't have one. Plus, we like to go target shooting.

ED

WISCONSIN

M1 Garand

As a history teacher, it's nice to have a tangible link to the past when I'm planning lectures on World War II, World War I, the Cold War, Vietnam. When you're trying to think what someone might have thought during a war, it's nice to be able to look at something that might have been there.

Jean and Fleming
Louisiana

Winchester .410 model 42

Fleming: I was born and raised 12 miles down the road from where Bonnie Parker and Clyde Barrow were ambushed and killed — this was in 1935. As a result of that incident, Northern Louisiana gained a reputation for being a very violent part of the world. And indeed, everybody — that I knew anyway — had at least two guns: a shotgun and a .22 rifle. But these weapons were looked upon mostly as implements for harvesting food, much like you do with hoes, rakes, shovels, and things like that. Because they were used to take wild game. And in a country at that time where there was no electricity, no trains to speak of, you couldn't buy anything. If you didn't grow it or kill it yourself, you didn't eat. So everybody that I knew of, went out to hunt for food and shells were expensive. It was on the edge of the depression, shortly before World War II and people learned to practice gun economy, I guess you would say. People took care of guns, guns were cherished ... and you didn't mess with somebody's gun. They were used as something to acquire food. That was all they were used for. This business about people shooting each other — that has come about, I think, as a result of money being introduced into our culture. Some people didn't have any, and some people wanted some, so they went out and "liberated" it.

Jean: I hate guns. Don't get me started.

JACOB
OREGON

Beretta 92F

At this point it's sort of unclear why I still have a gun. At the time I bought it, it was just something that all my friends were doing. We were just kind of like people that owned guns and went to the woods and shot stuff and blew things up. I think it was a period in my life when I was more interested in my rights, like, "Oh, I can vote and I can register for the draft and smoke cigarettes and look, I can buy guns." So I just ended up buying a gun.

ELIJAH WITH RUBY TUESDAY
NEW MEXICO

Ruger P90 - .45

I think guns are excellent tools. I appreciate the design of them. I appreciate their functionality. It's just the sort of thing I'm into.

MAGGIE AND GWEN
PENNSYLVANIA

Marlin .22, KelTec P-11, Kimber Pro-Carry .45

Gwen: I find shooting enjoyable, but I also own guns for self-defense, against criminals of all sorts, including those who single out minorities. Being a survivor of sexual assault, I find comfort in being able to take back the strength that was stolen from me by force. Arming myself equalizes force levels between an attacker and myself, giving me a fighting chance should someone once again decide to take what I do not wish to give.

We each have the right to be the source of our own salvation from evil if we so choose. That right must not be usurped by those who would run our lives for us according to their own agendas, whether it be for the basest of self-interests, or for the noblest of altruisms.

Maggie: Well, my reasons are pretty much the same as Gwen's which she expressed very well — save that I've never been the victim of sexual assault myself.

H.T.

CALIFORNIA

Colt Python, Colt M1917, SW M29, SW M1955 Target

I own guns for the same reason that I own fast cars and fast motorcycles. Something about the mechanical aspect of riding, and driving, and shooting, and tinkering with these machines that appeals to me. They appeal to me — that's pretty much it.

JASON AND HEATHER
ARIZONA

Ruger Sp101, HK P7M8,

Jason: I wasn't allowed to have toy guns as a kid.

Heather: I have a gun so that I can take care of myself. So that I don't have to worry about being a victim. So that I can have fun and go shooting with my husband and my friends who shoot, and because I don't think it's something that should be forbidden to anybody.

JAMES

PENNSYLVANIA

Stoeger Condor 12 Gauge Over and Under

I'm not really interested in guns. I don't particularly like them. But I was commissioned to sculpt a duck hunter, an interesting figure. Rather than make a gun out of clay, I just bought this Citori knockoff and made a mold from it. The bronze cast is in Missouri now. I reclaimed the body of the statue and I'm making something else out of it now. The gun's been in a paper bag in my closet for years.

H.W.

MASSACHUSETTS

Para Ordinance High Capacity .45

The thing that really stimulated my getting a firearm was my grandfather's interest. Behind every door in his house there was a gun and all these mounted heads on the wall. You might say there was a graphic reminder of aspirated anxiety everywhere. When I was a young child, I remember him sitting at the dining room table with my father and in front of him was a Colt New Service Revolver. It's a very large heavy-duty weapon, the largest revolver around at the time. My grandfather said to my father: "If you have any trouble with this kid, just send me over and I'll take care of him." He had a certain way of frightening people. I felt I really wasn't safe unless I had the same gun. I got one when I turned 18 and I felt a lot better because I was no longer afraid of my grandfather.

NICK, JENNIE, RANDI WITH SAM AND DUDE
WISCONSIN

Mossberg 12 guage, Remington 870, Remington Fieldmaster

Nick: I don't have my own gun right now. I'm hoping to pick one out soon. Until then, I'm borrowing one.

Jennie: We live out in the country. We hunt deer a lot. My father owned guns all of his life. I grew up with them, so I have guns. My first experience was shooting a double barreled shotgun in the swamps of Louisiana. I dang near fell over.

Randi: I got my gun for Christmas. I was a little afraid to shoot it. I was worried that it was going to kick. In hunter safety they gave me some softer shells that kick less. We learned blood tracking. We followed fake blood and they hid a deer head and skin behind a tree, and I screamed when I found it.

JAMES
LOUISIANA

Perazzi MX2000

I've been a gun maker for 35 years. I own guns because I'm free. Freedom is taken, never given.

RODNEY AND KRIS WITH REX

Ruger Redhawk .41 magnum

Rodney: It's fun to go out and see how accurate I can be, with a pistol or a rifle. To be able to put the sights on target, to put it where I want it. That's discipline.

JON WITH CHARLES GREY AND JENNY LIND
KENTUCKY

Street Sweeper 12 gauge, Reproduction 1858 Remington New Army - .44 cal

In the military I found out that I was a very good shot and I decided to keep up with it after I got out. I've had a whole series of guns. I enjoy them. I enjoy firing them. I enjoy the target practice.

JEREMY WITH CHARLOTTE
WISCONSIN

Stevens Model 58 12 gauge

This was my father's shotgun. He hunted with it with his father. I do hunt, but not very often. It's a stomach issue, not a morality issue. I guess I just don't like to know where my meat comes from. Occasionally my son and I will go down to the dump and shoot bottles and cans.

GWEN, JEP AND DIANA WITH LILLY
PENNSYLVANIA

Springfield M1A with Eotech HWS EBR, Remington 870 Police Magnum with Surefire front end, Colt Anaconda

Jep: The "Gun Culture" is an enormous part of my heritage. It has become part of my wife's throughout the past 23 years we have been best friends. It will be a part of our children's heritage as well, so long as we can protect it. It has nothing to do with violence. In fact, it has much to do with just the opposite. It's about bringing people together. Shooting is a great way to spend time with family and friends.

We also believe fervently in the sovereignty of the individual and the family unit. We are citizens, with inalienable rights, not subjects to be ruled. Our right to keep and bear arms comes from our Bill of Rights, and this right, as enumerated, is not granted by any local, state or federal authority. It is a recognized right, endowed by our creator, upon every freeborn citizen in this country. The right to keep and bear arms isn't so that the citizens can hunt or target shoot. It is recognized so that they may protect this country, their state, their community, their families and themselves against those that wish to do them harm, be it a foreign enemy, their own government, or some thug.

JOSEPH

PENNSYLVANIA

Remington Model 700 7mm Magnum

The first time I was introduced to guns was when I was hunting with my dad, grandfather, and uncle. I remember my dad shooting a ringneck pheasant and a rabbit. I carried those two animals until I thought my arms were going to fall off. That made a great impression on me. I've hunted all of my life. I have a tremendous respect for life, especially wildlife. It never ceases to amaze me how much satisfaction I get from just simply being in the Great Outdoors, whether I make a kill or not.

MICHELLE AND KYLE
MISSOURI

Glock 17, Remington 870

Kyle: There are too many idiots who own guns. I have major problems with some parts of the firearm culture. I've met completely irresponsible gun owners who do a good job of making the rest of us look bad. They don't seem to understand the serious responsibility that you take on when you own and operate firearms.

I've made it my mission to take as many people out to the range as I can to raise interest and add more responsible firearm owners to our society. I constantly preach the importance of taking a safety course and developing good habits from the start. Also, since the majority of my friends are politically liberal, I'm trying to do my part to break through this very ridiculous partisan split over gun rights.

And, of course, firearms are a great defense against non-stationary cadavers if my neighborhood ever becomes the victim of a zombie infestation.

Michelle: I'm not really "into" guns. I own one because there are guns in the house and I figured I should know how to use them.

KEVIN WITH BUDDY
KENTUCKY

(holding) 146LD: FN-RS 2000 - (clockwise from left) AR-15, M1Garand, HK MP5 (full auto) HK USP - .40 R, ACC Evolution - .40 SW, Glock 19, AA Evolution 9mm, RAC Phantom - .22LR, HK USP .45, AAC Evolution - .45, Remington 870, GGG 45, Bulldog Terminator, Remington 700 PSS

As a Jewish American I am cognizant of the fact that 6 million of my people were turned into air pollution in the '30s and '40s. As a civil rights advocate I know that at some point words are not going to be enough when people are kicking down your door to pull you out of your house because you're Jewish, or black, or gay. You can't be pro civil rights without being pro gun. It's hypocritical to deny someone the most basic of all human rights, which is the right to defend yourself.

John with Gunther

*Winchester Model 52 Target rifle .22 caliber with palm-rest and adjustable butt-plate/shoulder horn and
J.Unertl optical scope*

I started shooting six years ago to get my mind off of things when my wife passed away. I do competitive bulls-eye shooting with three handguns, and outdoors at 200 yards with a rifle. At my age you can't compete in team sports any more, so now it's you against yourself. That's it. I punch holes in paper.

DEVIN AND KEVIN
TEXAS

Henry replica

Kevin: The only weapons I've ever owned, aside from my duty weapon, were sporting arms: rifles and shotguns. No semi-autos that could be converted to full auto. There's no need for that. Hunting and fishing, a love for the outdoors — that's how I was raised.

KENYATTA
PENNSYLVANIA

Taurus PT40

I don't wear sports jerseys. I only wear sneakers to the gym and I don't know many of the latest rap artists. Instead I smoke cigars, enjoy wine tasting and like to travel. I enjoy my gun ownership on many levels that many people may not expect when they see my face.

I grew up in the heart of West Philadelphia — 45th and Westminster. It still is pretty rough around there. You see a lot of violence which has more to do with the people who were getting the guns and not the guns themselves. My mother raised us well so I have that foundation, but I also have a bit of realism in me. Sometimes you need a little protection for yourself, even as you move out of the city and acquire nice things. I have a Mercedes out in the driveway — sometimes I get some eyes and I like to have a little protection on me.

I enjoy the camaraderie of shooting at the range. I enjoy the history of guns and gun makers. And of course the sense of security that comes with owning and knowing how to properly use a firearm. It's a privilege and responsibility that I take very seriously.

KATE, PETE AND LORI WITH HEIDI
MISSOURI

Rock River Arms AR-15

Pete: The Second Amendment isn't about duck hunting. It's about owning firearms that are serious enough to keep the government honest.

Lori: I've got a gun because he likes guns.

MARK AND LORI
OREGON

HK MP5, Uzi (both full auto)

Mark: We take our gun ownership and our Second Amendment rights pretty seriously. I'm not a religious person, but I suppose if you had to ask me what I have strong convictions about — the power of ownership and the ability to own firearms, to responsibly own them and use them — is up there at the top of my list. I think for me a big part of owning guns is a reflection of freedom in our country. A government that doesn't respect its citizens enough to responsibly own firearms is a government probably not to be trusted and maybe even to be feared. I think of the Second Amendment as kind of the reset button to the Constitution. When the others start to fail, then it's time to look to it for redress.

Lori: I think it's important that people understand firearms. If you respect them and understand how to handle them then you won't be afraid of them — that they won't jump up off the table and go rob the nearest 7-11. That you will be able to instill in your family, your friends, your children, a respect for them. A healthy respect. And that's the key.

KEVIN

WISCONSIN

Springfield Armory XD-40 Tactical

First and foremost I own guns because I can. The right to own a firearm is very important and something I cherish. I own guns because I hunt. Self-defense is secondary; though it's important. In my state, people aren't allowed to carry concealed. I can carry a firearm; I'm a deputy sheriff, but common citizens can't carry concealed.

IVY AND KIT WITH AUTUMN
NEW JERSEY

W. Roberts 12 gauge, Browning over-and-under

Ivy: I grew up on a farm, and I can't remember an age when I wasn't around guns. It was always clear to me that I was not to touch one without permission, but I was encouraged to learn to use them, and taught that shooting guns is an acceptable recreational activity. I've never hunted. It would be easier for me to shoot a person breaking into my home than it would be to kill an animal whose home I'd invaded.

Kit: My grandfather gave me my first shotgun when I was 8. He taught us how to shoot. I don't think that I could ever kill anything, but I enjoy shooting at targets. Having grown up in Texas in a family where firearms were common, I never considered it out of place to have a gun in the house. I firmly believe that it's every citizen's right to own guns, and their responsibility to treat them with respect. Anything can be dangerous if misused.

MIKE
OREGON

Benelli Nova 12 ga.

I'm a chef. Two years ago I realized that I wanted to shoot, cook and eat a wild turkey for Thanksgiving: the ultimate free-range bird. It was one of the best meals of my life. The whole thing, everything added up to a wonderful experience. It's hard to describe, but it's a lot different when you actually have to pluck the feathers and reach your hand into the warm body and pull out the guts, rather than just slicing up a pre-frozen package that's wrapped and sanitized for your protection. It's a lot more intimate, a lot higher quality, a lot better flavor.

PORTIA AND ANTHONY WITH YUMI AND LEELOODALLASMULTIPASS
PENNSYLVANIA

Beretta 96, Remington 870

Portia: I learned to shoot a gun when I was 10 or 11. My mother had a boyfriend who was a San Luis Obispo County Sheriff. He lived in a teepee with a "wolf dog." We'd stay out there, eat ashcakes for breakfast and shoot his guns. The first time I shot a shotgun, I landed on my ass and laughed uncontrollably the way you do when you're a kid.

Anthony: I own a gun because I'm a fuckin' American and a Marine. It's my God-given right.

MIKE
FLORIDA

HK USP 40, Mossberg 590

I own guns because I like them. And because I can.

PATRICK
PENNSYLVANIA

44/40

I grew up in a country where guns were strictly illegal. Bullets were actually illegal, too. You could get prison time for every single bullet you had on you. And growing up there I was always fascinated with the American cowboy and the cowboy's sense of fair play, justice and self-reliance. If a cowboy was wronged or slighted or attacked or robbed, he didn't call 911 and wait for somebody else to come and save his bacon. He handled the situation himself.

I feel that it's not so much a right, but almost a responsibility to be able to defend myself and the people that rely on me and care about me, and that I care about, in the event of some sort of breakdown of public and civil order here, the way we did with hurricane Katrina in New Orleans. I want to make sure that I'm protected and the people with me are protected, too.

Matt and Lisa with Arthur
Rhode Island

Ruger 10/22

Matt: Shooting targets is fun but the more practical reason is that I have locks on my doors, and a fire extinguisher and a smoke detector and a first aid kit and a carbon monoxide detector. It always struck me as a logical extension of that — guns are one more thing that people should have for preparedness.

Lisa: I own a gun because I grew up hunting and I got one as a present from my dad when I was 18 so I could go target shooting. It never really occurred to me not to have one.

RALPH

Danish Krag, AK-47, C.C. Smithe 12 Ga, Colt Government Model .45, and Walther P38

I keep this Danish Krag rifle as a reminder of my father-in-law who fought in the Danish underground in WWII. The AK-47 — I bought that for my son, when he was in the Paras, so that he could learn to use the enemy's weapon if he ever had to. The Colt .45 pistol is for "PLP" — Protection of Life and Property. The P38 I keep as a reminder of a fellow I worked with years ago who served in WWII. I have other guns because, having been an engineer and a machinist, I'm always interested in the mechanics of guns. Over the years as well I've lived in some of the garden spots of the world and had to carry a gun, so I do appreciate them.

TIA AND STEVE WITH ANUBIS, LUCY AND OMEN
FLORIDA

Bersa Thunder .380 stainless, Beretta 92fs 9mm, Glock 22 10mm

Steve: A good buddy of mine was a gun carrier and always told me I should carry a gun: *Things can happen.* I said "What the heck, okay." Luckily, I haven't had to use it. It got pretty close a couple of times.

Tia: I lived by myself in an apartment. It was needed. It's not safe for a girl anymore.

MIKE WITH LINUS
OREGON

Valmet M88 AK-47, Mossberg 12 gauge

I am a liberal Democrat and many of my friends are suprised to find that I'm a gun owner. They have this idea that gun owners are all a bunch of rednecks out in the woods poaching deer, but we're all over the spectrum, not some monoculture. My primary reason for owning weapons is self-defense. Also because it's a duty as a citizen to be able to defend not only my home, but my neighborhood if I have to. I agree with John Locke's theory that if we have people who are armed, and who carry concealed and are responsible, that's going to cut down on violent crime. I carry concealed and I've taken the time and the pains to make sure I know how to handle my firearm if I have to. It's something I hope never happens. I don't want to go to jail. I don't want to get sued. I don't want to face prosecution. I just want that last resort in case I have to use it.

BROTHER ROBB
OHIO

Remington 870 Home Defense 12 Gauge, Savage 7mm Rem. Mag (w/scope), Sig Sauer 2340 (.40S&W), Springfield Armory XD .45ACP (gold slide), Glock 22 (.40S&W), Browning Buckmark, Yugoslavian SKS (7.62x39), CZ 75 P-01 (9mm), New English Translation (NET) Bible

I'm from Indiana. The subculture there is not a subculture. It's the predominant culture. But I was never into guns until I saw *Bowling for Columbine*. It seemed to attempt to demonize an inanimate object, and I don't think you can do that with something that doesn't think, feel, or understand the concept of morality. I understand why people have an emotional reaction to things that are bad: murder and robbery, for example. It got me thinking and anyway, after the movie some friends and I went to a local target range to experience it first hand — to see what all the hype was about. It was a spark. After that, I bought two pistols.

LIBERTY AND MICHAEL WITH GENERAL BEAUREGARD
FLORIDA

SVT40, Finnish M1938, Uzi 9mm, AK-47

Michael: A gun is capable of performing tremendously "good" acts or tremendously "evil" acts. And I see this as an analogy of human beings — we can do good or we can do evil. As an American I believe it's my natural right to own a firearm, guaranteed in the Constitution. As a Jew, I believe history has shown we have been victimized for 2,000 years and to some extent that victimization has been allowed by us because we did not have the means to resist. One thing I'm sadly aware of after studying the Holocaust is that if those individuals had the means to defend themselves, they more than likely would have done so and perhaps the Holocaust would have gone a different way.

Basically we own firearms for utilitarian reasons — no better word than that. I shoot every Friday, but we're also using them for defense. Occasionally things go bad down here. This house was totally destroyed by hurricane Andrew and then it was damaged by hurricanes Katrina and Wilma and the guns came out for that. I sat out there in the front yard after Wilma. Me and the neighbors stood out there collectively and made sure that nothing happened. I'm not sure if the guns prevented anything from happening, but if something did, they were there.

ROBERT WITH DOBRO
TEXAS

Springfield M1A

I've owned and shot firearms for as long as I can remember. I grew up hunting and shooting with my family and I continue that tradition to this day.

However, the Second Amendment to the Constitution was not drafted to safeguard the rights of hunters or target shooters to practice their avocation. The Second Amendment exists as one of the most fundamental checks and balances in our republic: a check by the citizenry against the very real possibility of a tyrannical government that ceases to be subject to the concerted will of the people. This country was born from armed rebellion and we must protect that right as a last resort for securing and maintaining our hard won liberty. I feel it's the duty of every citizen of the United States of America to maintain a proficiency at arms in order to defend the republic against all enemies, foreign and domestic. That includes ones own government should it become necessary.

To quote Colonel Jeff Cooper: "Pick up a rifle and you change instantly from a subject to a citizen."

NICKY

Colt AR-15

I have 32 handguns and 17 long arms. I'm not a collector. I just love to purchase firearms. I don't know if I could choose — between my guns and my motorcycle.

STAN

PENNSYLVANIA

Taurus PT 38S, .38 Super

It's a right and a privilege. Everybody should exercise it. I think everybody should have a gun. It levels the playing field.

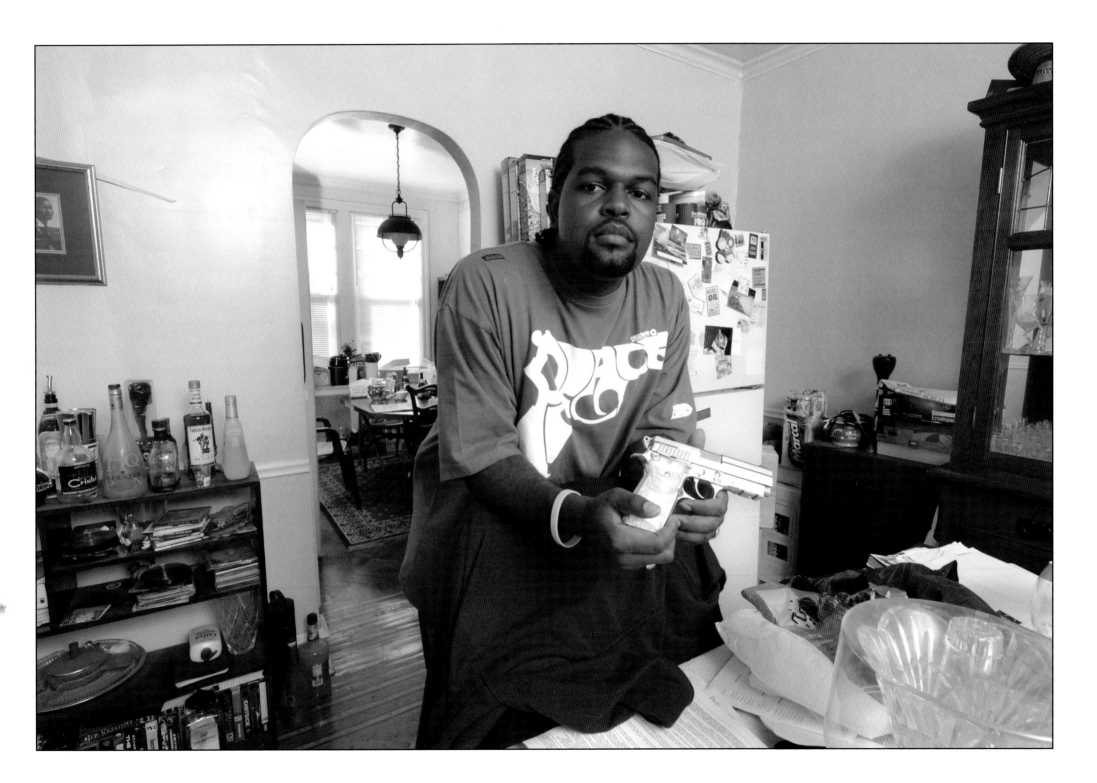

GAIL, ERIC, MORGAN AND MICHAEL WITH MISTY

Cricket .22, M4 Carbine, Mondo AR-15

Michael: I'm a reservist. I need to maintain proficiency and we only practice once a year, so any extra training I can get, especially with military weapons, is better for me if we deploy. I sometimes carry a handgun when I travel. There are always areas where you feel more comfortable if you have some form of defense on hand. You can't avoid everything. I'm puzzled when I run into people who are adamantly opposed to the concept.

Gail: I'm not really into guns, but they're in the house and I know how to use them. I'm in the military right now. I hope that I'll never have to put a person at the other end of one, but if I do, it's because it's me or them, and I'm going to choose me.

Morgan: I like shooting. Mom helps me.

Eric: I shoot targets. And bows and arrows.

Ochressandro

New Mexico

Romarm SSg-97(PSL) and Maadi AK-47

As the Founding Fathers said, sometimes the tree of liberty must be watered with the blood of tyrants and patriots. If that day comes, I will be ready, to defend my country against all threats, domestic and foreign. I have sworn eternal enmity to the forces of socialism and control. I own firearms, and have drilled myself to proficiency with their use because I have read *Gulag Archipelago*, and I will not let it happen here without a fight.

Advocates of gun control think that they will someday take my arms from me. But they are wrong. I'll own guns all my life.

NEAL, OWEN AND LORA WITH BRANDY

Henry N. Hooper M 1857 12 Pound Napoleon, .22 Sharps Derringer

Neal: This fascination started when I was a kid — watching movies and stuff like that. As I grew older I was able to get them legally so I started getting historical weapons. Primarily I collect antiques and historical arms.

Lora: Guilt by association, sort of. I grew up with them. They were always here and going to the shooting competitions was what my dad did, so I went out and did what my dad did. I went out and shot Civil War shooting competitions. It was family time with Dad.

Owen: This is my grandfather's musket. He used to shoot with it in competitions and handed that down to me. Growing up around guns like I did, I just got used to them. I'm comfortable around them and I'm fascinated with the power and what they can do.

RICHARD
OREGON

Smith and Wesson 642 Airweight .38 Special

I love firearms. As long as I can remember, I've wanted to own one. I first started shooting in Boy Scouts with a .22 rifle years and years ago and I was just hooked ever since. When I turned 21, I bought a gun for self-defense, got the permit and I've carried ever since. I have a few firearms: a rifle that a buddy gave to me for Christmas; I have a training gun; a couple of replicas; an AK-47. Hopefully the collection will keep going on.

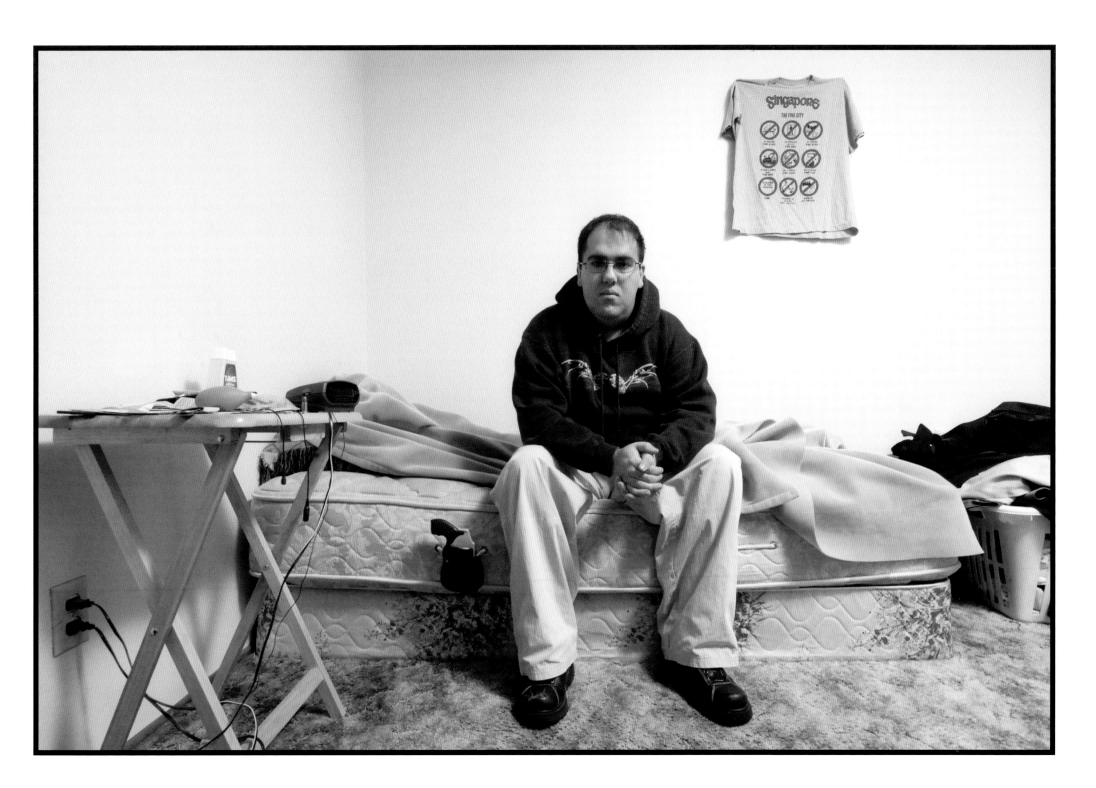

DAVID, KRYSTLE, NOEL, KASSANDRA AND KINDRA
PENNSYLVANIA

H+R 12 guage, Traditions Flintlock .50, Springfield XD9, Glock 17 9mm

David: Hunting is my main purpose — time in the woods. Mostly it's just quiet time walking in the woods. I can be out there for hours and hours.

Krystle: I own a gun mainly for hunting. I grew up around guns, grew up with my Pop-Pop target shooting with me at the cabin, and shooting with my dad. He was the one who got me my very first .22. I started plinking with that — grew to love it. Then got my first deer with my Russian rifle, then moved along to the muzzle loaders, then archery; but hunting's my main thing. I've shot three deer. The last one with this flintlock. It didn't even take a step after I shot. It just fell over.

Noel: I used to hate guns; they scared me — the usual "guns kill". Then my husband took me out to the range and I enjoyed it. Then we started going with our friends. My thinking changed a lot. It's not the guns that kill, it's the people that kill. When the kids were younger, I wasn't sure I wanted anything dangerous in the house. Then I realized there were plenty of things in the house more dangerous than an unloaded gun. I feel pretty good about them now. I just love to shoot.

Kindra: I go shooting at least once a week with my family. I don't like big guns — they kick too hard. I usually shoot my dad's Glock with the .22 barrel on it, and every now and then I'll switch to 9mm. I like shooting. My sisters and I used to shoot my sister's BB gun in the basement. Krystle always used to be a better shot, but now I can out-shoot her so I like to rub it in her face.

Kassandra: I have nothing against guns, but I have never had an urge to shoot any of them. I still think they're cool and I love that we have them in the house. My friends are all really impressed by the collection.

Steven
Missouri

Smith and Wesson .38 Special

I always liked fireworks as a kid and these are like fireworks for adults. It's completely gluttonous on my behalf. I really like handguns, although I do find them ultimately frivolous. It's like cars. I love cars. I don't need a car, I could live without a car, but I own two cars and a motorcycle because I like them. And I own three guns. I really enjoy the mechanics of them. I like firing them.

SONYA AND TODD
FLORIDA

Uzi SMG, Mini Uzi SMG, Beretta 92

Todd: I never thought I would need or want a firearm until in 2002 I was told by law enforcement during a community outreach program that in the event of a disaster such as a terrorist attack or a massive hurricane, they will not be able to protect everyone. People will have to fend for themselves. It seems like common sense now after what happened in New Orleans during hurricane Katrina, but I was naïve then and I thought the powers that be would always be there to keep law and order.

What started as my desire to be responsible and to protect my family has led to a passion for competitive pistol, rifle and submachine gun shooting. My initial notions of firearms were simply wrong; and they have changed as I have learned over the past several years. I now own a gun because I enjoy the shooting sports and because I will not allow my family or myself to be victimized by violence or tyranny.

I refuse to be prey.

Sonya: Even better than owning a gun and knowing how to use it is competing with it, so you know you can handle it correctly. With practice you get better at it. We both enjoy it. It's fun to get better together.

RY

Bushmaster XM15 E25 2006 SEBR

I own a gun because a disarmed populace is required for genocide and should it come around again, I'm not going to be that guy. I'm not going to be standing on the side.

BETH, PAUL, GAVIN AND EMMA
VIRGINIA

AK-47, Bersa .380, Ruger P345

Paul: My family had guns the whole time I was a kid. Then I went off and joined the Army and went away and came back. I have guns now largely for the same reason I have fire extinguishers in the house and spare tires in the car. I'm a self-reliant kind of guy and there could come a time when I need to protect my family.

Beth: I have one for self-protection. I was raised to never rely on anyone else to protect me or watch my back. It took me a year to pick out one that I liked.

TIM

Stephens single barrel 12 gauge

The reason I have a gun is because I grew up with them. I collect them. My dad collects them. I grew up hunting with my grandfather. Even my brother, we all grew up hunting. My brother's into self-defense. He has a concealed weapon permit. I believe in self-protection, but I hardly ever carry a gun. My brother don't leave the house without one. I'm not like that. I like to hunt. Some people collect candle holders; I collect weapons.

VICTORIA, CATHY AND RAPHAEL WITH ROMULUS AND REMUS
PENNSYLVANIA

M4 Carbine with scope

Raphael: I was a criminal justice major in college, and while I am a big supporter of law enforcement, I was always struck by how reactive law enforcement ultimately is. In other words, too often, crime has already been committed before law enforcement becomes involved. That sent me a strong and clear message. It is up to us, as citizens, to protect ourselves, our families and our property. Our constitution provides us with the right and the method by which to achieve that objective. I choose to exercise that right.

SEAN
FLORIDA

AK-47

I own a weapon because I really enjoy going to the range and shooting. I'm a Buddhist. I don't believe in violence and I don't believe in using a weapon for violence. But I think that when it comes down to the core essence of owning a gun, a gun isn't violent but the nature of a *person* can become violent. The biggest test is when someone is confronted and chooses to react with violence.

KRISTINE, REX AND LISA WITH RUSTY AND WHISKERS
PENNSYLVANIA

Glenfield Marlin Model 60 - .22 cal

Rex: I sometimes take it out and go target shooting. It's actually been in the attic for years.

Lisa: I did feel better having it in the house when Rex was on deployment.

TIMOTHY
WASHINGTON

Model 30 Glock, AR-15, 1770 flintlock

If there were two banks side by side and you knew one of the banks was full of people that carry guns, and the other bank had a sign that said "absolutely no guns allowed" and you knew that the area was a bad area, with the possibility of a robbery, which bank would you go to? The one that more than likely will be robbed, or the one that no way in the world would a robber go in there? That's one of the reasons that I carry a gun. I like the satisfaction of knowing that all odds are equal. Criminals shouldn't have guns, and when they do carry guns, it's illegal. When I carry a gun it's not and that's the important thing — that it's not illegal for good citizens and trained citizens to carry weapons.

Catie and Dan with Havoc
Missouri

STG 58

Catie: I met Dan and he was into guns. He took me shooting — I freaking loved it and I happen to be pretty good at it. It's always nice when a guy comes over and says "Wow! Who's target is that?"

Dan: Part of it's for protection, part of it's a hobby. I'm interested in history. A lot of the guns I own have some historical significance, even if they don't have a lot of monetary value. It's just interesting to own that and work with that type of stuff.

GAUGE AND SHANE WITH TATTOO
PENNSYLVANIA

Bushmaster AR-15 (modified to M-203), MAG-7 12 gauge shotgun, HK SL8 (modified to a G36), Mossberg 500, Saiga 12, Polytech AK-47, Thompson .45

I own guns for several reasons. I think initially it was my attraction to things that are "dangerous," things that are not necessarily seen as normal and acceptable, or things that a majority of others try to stay clear of. I started off with a Mossberg 500 12 gauge shotgun. I thought at the time that would be it. I shot it a few times and ended up diving head first into a new addiction. Now, several years later, I have an extensive collection of nearly 20 guns. Now that I'm a father, having guns in the house makes me feel more secure.

CRAIG WITH VIOLET
NORTH CAROLINA

Essex .410, Browning 12GA Semi

These guns belonged to my grandfather, my mother's father. He died in 1963 and left them to me. The Browning hasn't been fired in 40 years. I know the .410's been shot since then — my mother blew a hole in her living room wall with it in 1996. I hang onto them because it's all I've got to remember my grandfather. My camera now — they'll get that when they pry it from my cold, dead hands.

RICK, THOMAS AND SUE
WASHINGTON

Kimber Pro Carry Stainless II

Rick: Professionally, I'm a police officer and it's a necessary tool of the job. I enjoy shooting, but I practice a lot of combat arts. We do martial arts out of this house. I've been studying for years, and the pistol is like a Samurai sword to me. It's just one tool. To be proficient with a tool, you've got to train with it, so we do a lot of that in my profession. Gun ownership is simply a necessary aspect of what I do.

Valentine with Chomsky
Mississippi

M1 Carbine, M4, Colt 1911, Romanian SAR1, Various hand assembled AR-15s

I own firearms because I love freedom. Everyone is born free, just as they are born atheists. Freedom is something you assume and then you wait for someone to try to take it away. The degree to which we resist is the degree to which we are free.

I will defend my freedom against the real threat of our fascist police state of a government — not the fabricated threat of another country that has never invaded us. If you want to fight for your freedom, start here at home.

WAYNE WITH CLANCY AND TRIXIE

ARIZONA

Sig Sauer SHR 970 .30-06, Springfield Arms .45

I own a gun because an armed citizenry is the best defense against tyranny. I also just like to shoot.

RYAN AND ZACH
OREGON

Ruger M77 MkII .30-06, Stevens .30-30

Zach: I own a gun because gun ownership is the bedrock of our democracy, and in my opinion, people who benefit from our democracy should be willing to defend it, and that may include the use of firearms to do that, both from enemies foreign and domestic.

Ryan: I own a gun because I'm interested in all aspects of life, and gun ownership is certainly one which I'm curious about and want to know, from all aspects — hunting, protection, whatever. I had vague notions of starting up hunting. There's always time for that, I suppose, at some point. And then at least I have it if the day comes when it needs to be used for whatever reason. I don't know if that day will ever come, but I'll have that option.

DAN
OREGON

Smith and Wesson 681, FN Forty-Nine .40, Broomhandle Mauser 9x19 Ruger

I own guns because they're neat. Some people collect stamps. I ended up with a gun collection. They're all fun in their own special way. The sheer joy of one-handing the Bushmaster XM18 makes you feel like Robocop when you're shooting toilets out in the middle of nowhere. The cold precision of something like the 10/22 with a scope where you can knock out the head on a coin — a Canadian coin, of course, because defacing American currency is a crime — the feel, the action, the smell… People who tend to want to do away with guns, I think, are people who are insecure with making their own decisions. The mark of a free society is one where you don't think what could go wrong and make laws based on that, but you realize that there will *always* be negative consequences to everything and you take the bad with the good — otherwise everything would be getting outlawed.

Jessica, Gregg and Ben with Bubba
Wisconsin

Kentuckian Muzzle loader replica, Beretta Urika, Mendoza air rifle

Gregg: My primary reason for owning a gun is for sporting use. I really enjoy hunting all types of game from bear to deer to small game. I really enjoy target shooting, too. Now that I have two small children we really enjoy just going out and plinking. It's a great family activity. I think it teaches our kids responsibility. They're learning things about discipline and responsibility that they might not learn otherwise.

WILLIAM AND JENNIFER WITH BUDDAH
MISSOURI

AK-47, Walther P22

William: I could say it's for protection. I could say I enjoy the sport of shooting. I could even say that guns are an investment and, in fact, that would all be true. But honestly I own guns because they look cool. It probably has a lot to do with G.I. Joe.

Jennifer: I own guns for two reasons. First, I enjoy target shooting. I like to challenge myself. Second, there are guns in our society and I want to be confident in my ability to safely handle them in any situation.

WYLIE
TEXAS

FN-FAL

I'm a patriotic American and I believe it is the duty of every patriotic American to be able to hit a man-sized target at 250 yards.

JESSICA WITH SAMANTHA
NORTH CAROLINA

Kahr P9

I'm just one little girl in the world.

ELANOR AND DREW WITH OBIE
NEW JERSEY

SKS 776, 1958 .22 cal Single Bolt Action, Mossberg Single shot 12g, Mossberg 12g pump, Ruger P90 .45 cal

Drew: Owning a firearm brings me some sort of balance. When I am angry at the world I find relief in dropping a clip into the air. And, at the same time, if the world threatens me or those I love, I find relief in the protection it gives me.

JAMES WITH NICKY
PENNSYLVANIA

Taurus .38 snub nose special, Colt 380-Auto, Pony Pocketlite, Sig Sauer P232 .380

When I was diagnosed with cancer I found myself and my family in need of protection. I was too old to fight, too sick to run, and since cancer took my vocal cords, I couldn't yell for help. I purchased my first firearm.